What Makes Things Go?

THIS EDITION
Editorial Management by Oriel Square
Produced for DK by WonderLab Group LLC
Jennifer Emmett, Erica Green, Kate Hale, *Founders*

Editors Grace Hill Smith, Libby Romero, Michaela Weglinski;
Photography Editors Kelley Miller, Annette Kiesow, Nicole DiMella;
Managing Editor Rachel Houghton; **Designers** Project Design Company;
Researcher Michelle Harris; **Copy Editor** Lori Merritt; **Indexer** Connie Binder; **Proofreader** Larry Shea;
Reading Specialist Dr. Jennifer Albro; **Curriculum Specialist** Elaine Larson

Published in the United States by DK Publishing
1745 Broadway, 20th Floor, New York, NY 10019

Copyright © 2023 Dorling Kindersley Limited
DK, a Division of Penguin Random House LLC
23 24 25 26 10 9 8 7 6 5 4 3 2 1
001-333895-June/2023

All rights reserved.

Without limiting the rights under the copyright reserved above, no part of this publication may be reproduced, stored in or introduced into a retrieval system, or transmitted, in any form, or by any means (electronic, mechanical, photocopying, recording, or otherwise), without the prior written permission of the copyright owner.
Published in Great Britain by Dorling Kindersley Limited

A catalog record for this book
is available from the Library of Congress.
HC ISBN: 978-0-7440-7185-6
PB ISBN: 978-0-7440-7186-3

DK books are available at special discounts when purchased in bulk for sales promotions, premiums, fundraising, or educational use. For details, contact: DK Publishing Special Markets,
1745 Broadway, 20th Floor, New York, NY 10019
SpecialSales@dk.com

Printed and bound in China

The publisher would like to thank the following for their kind permission to reproduce their images:
a=above; c=center; b=below; l=left; r=right; t=top; b/g=background

Dreamstime.com: Lev Akhsanov 11bl, Brad Calkins 19bl, Damedeeso 9bc, 17br, Torian Dixon 27br, Papp Dorottya 31tl, Fizkes 25br, Vladislav Gajic 14-15, Kelpfish 16crb, Iurii Kosintcev 18br, Dusan Kostic 16-17, Vladimir Melnikov 31clb, Sergey Novikov 24br, Michael Pettigrew 17bl, Romrodinka 6-7, Rtrembly 15bl, Shangarey 28-29, Pamela Uyttendaele 22br, Verkoka 8br; **Getty Images / iStock:** AndreyPopov 23bc, atusgk 26-27, E+ / Lorado 10-11, E+ / M_a_y_a 12br, E+ / real444 18-19, E+ / SanyaSM 13bl, E+ / South_agency 1cb, E+ / THEPALMER 30, jacoblund 7bl, kiankhoon 31bl, monkeybusinessimages 4-5, Photodisc / Ryan McVay 12-13, SerrNovik 20-21, Wavebreakmedia 24-25, XiXinXing 8-9; **Shutterstock.com:** Anatoliy Karlyuk 19br, Ljupco Smokovski 6bc, Studio.G photography 22-23, 31cl, Kent Weakley 20bc

Cover images: *Front:* **Getty Images / iStock:** E+ / Lorado bl, br; **Shutterstock.com:** hamlet_ggl tl, Receh Lancar Jaya ca, Anna Leskinen b/g Macrovector tr; *Back:* **123RF.com:** seamartini clb, **Dreamstime.com:** Sergey Siz`kov cla;
Spine: **Getty Images / iStock:** E+ / Lorado

All other images © Dorling Kindersley Limited
For more information see: www.dkimages.com

For the curious
www.dk.com

What Makes Things Go?

Libby Romero

What makes things go? Let's find out!

A push makes this toy car go.

push

7

A pull makes this snow tube move.

pull

8

Forces make things move.
A push is a force.
A pull is a force, too.

move

11

A strong force makes things go fast!

strong

Some forces make things slow down.

slow down

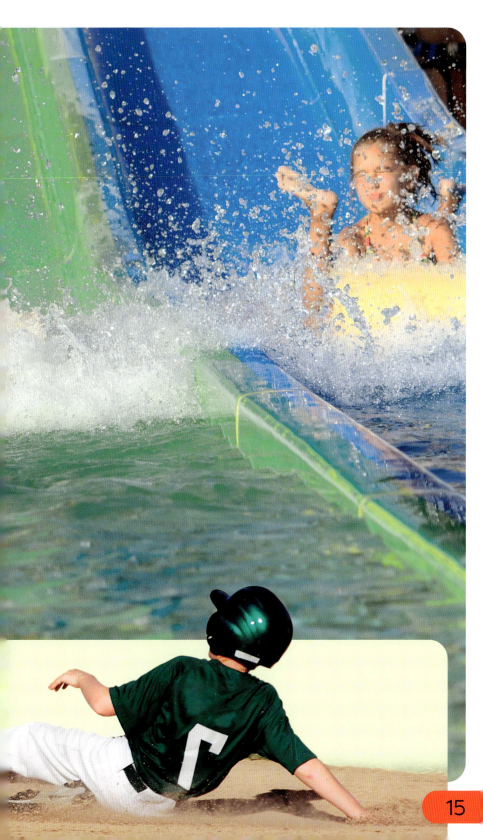

Some forces make things stop moving.

stop moving

Forces can make things change direction, too.

direction

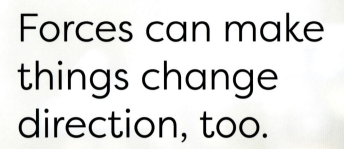

19

Forces make things move all around you. Wind pushes this kite up in the sky.

wind

Magnets pull these toy trains together.

magnets

circles

24

These people move their bodies.
They push and pull the hula hoops in circles!

25

force

Do you want to make something go? Apply force!

It takes a force to make objects move.

force

You use forces every day. Forces help make things go!

Glossary

direction
the way in which you face or travel

force
a push or a pull; using power to make something move

magnets
objects that pull things made of iron toward themselves.

pull
a type of force; moving something to bring it back toward you

push
a type of force; to move forward, down, or away from you

Quiz

Answer the questions to see what you have learned. Check your answers with an adult.

1. What are two kinds of forces?
2. What do forces make things do?
3. How do forces affect how things move? Give three examples.
4. True or False: A magnet can pull things together.
5. What is something you can apply force to? How would you move it?

1. Push and pull 2. Move 3. Make things go fast, make things slow down, make things stop moving 4. True 5. Answers will vary